Pastoral Care in Parishes Without a Pastor

Applications of Canon 517, §2

Barbara Anne Cusack

Therese Guerin Sullivan, S.P.

Pastoral Care in Parishes Without a Pastor

Applications of Canon 517, §2

Canon Law Society of America

Contents

Introduction

With its promulgation on January 25, 1983 the revised Code of Canon Law for the Latin Church came to life in the Church. In the more than ten years hence, the Church has, with more or less success, responded to the challenges of approaching the law with a "new way of thinking."[1] It may be when we are confronted with new ecclesiastical institutions that we most easily recognize the need for this new mind-set. Changing conditions call for new ways of approaching our mission as Church.

The newly introduced canon 517, §2 is a clear example of an effort to respond to new and different challenges in the Church. With the realization that declining numbers of priests will affect the form and structure of parish ministry and pastoral care, an innovative approach has been introduced in this canon. Canon 517, §2 states:

If the diocesan bishop should decide that due to a dearth of priests a participation in the exercise of the pastoral care of a parish is to be entrusted to a deacon or to some other person who is not a priest or to a community of persons, he is to appoint some priest endowed with the powers and faculties of a pastor to supervise the pastoral care.

1. Pope Paul VI, during the period of revision of the code, referred to the *"novus habitus mentis,"* a "new way of thinking" about the role of law in the Church. The expression is representative of a new approach towards the understanding of the function of law in the Church.

While this canon opens the door to a new style of parochial ministry, the law does not provide a well-defined plan for applying and implementing this canon. This is well and good! The variations among local churches throughout the world are such that a universal plan of action would hardly be applicable. Local culture, customs, concerns must help to shape the direction that implementation of canon 517, §2 will take.

The years since the promulgation of the 1983 code have seen dioceses move more or less slowly in applying canon 517, §2 to their local situations. Those dioceses which acted more quickly out of pressing need for this alternate form of pastoral care provided the ground-breaking and foundation-laying steps for other dioceses to consider. Practical issues needing attention have arisen as the new models for parish ministry have been built and re-built on the diocesan level. With more than ten years of experience with this alternate parish format, sociologists have had the opportunity to study trends and impacts. The successes and failures have been adequately documented in the literature on this topic! Several of the sources cited in the select annotated bibliography summarize results based on experience.

Theological reflections have presented further challenges in the movement to implement this provision for pastoral care. We need to balance the practicality of this implementation with consideration of its deeper implications, especially regarding Eucharistic celebrations as opposed to Celebrations of the Word or Communion services. What is intended as an "interim measure" could evolve into a common practice in some areas without sufficient reflection on the long term impact on the theology of ordained ministry, Eucharistic theology, and ecclesiology. While these theological issues are significant and cannot be ignored, their discussion is beyond the scope of this present project.

In May 1992, the Board of Governors of the Canon Law Society of America assigned to their Committee on Lay Ministry Research[2] the task of studying canon 517, §2. The goal was to sur-

2. Members of the Committee on Lay Ministry Research involved in this pro-

vey what applications were in place within the United States and also to propose some canonical considerations that dioceses might take into account when considering future directions in this regard. At times, pragmatic approaches to pressing needs have led to the establishment of policies and structures that do not take sufficient account of canonical norms and protections. The purpose of the committee's work was to propose some standards in the implementation of canon 517, §2 which would be firmly grounded canonically and still allow for needed local adaptation.

The variations in the application of canon 517, §2 throughout the United States quickly become apparent through even a cursory review of the documentation published by dioceses on this topic. The first fact that stands out is that the personnel involved in this new model have no consistent name or title! Position descriptions, responsibilities, qualifications, expectations, and accountability vary greatly from diocese to diocese. Canon law does not provide a solution to either dilemma. The law does not name the person to whom the bishop entrusts a "participation in the exercise of the pastoral care of a parish" nor the priest who is to "supervise the pastoral care." The law does not detail the scope or content of the pastoral care or the supervision. The code is silent on procedures and practices, often its bailiwick, where this new ecclesiastical institute is concerned.

In an effort to serve local dioceses in their application of canon 517, §2, the CLSA Committee on Lay Ministry Research has by analogy and interpretation drawn out some practical applications of canon 517, §2. The committee has chosen to address some broad issues such as position descriptions and procedures and to provide some concrete examples of documents that, while fulfilling canonical norms where necessary, might be adapted still further to address local needs.

Several choices were made by the committee in the course of

ject were: Dr. Barbara Anne Cusack, Mr. Robert Kampine, Reverend Jay Maddock, and Sr. Therese Guerin Sullivan, S.P. The committee is grateful to those who have reviewed these materials in their various stages and offered insight from their own experience and expertise.

its work. First, the committee elected to concentrate its concerns on the application of canon 517, §2 to lay persons. This decision is not meant to deny the place of permanent deacons in this new model, but rather to comply with the nature and purpose of this particular committee.

Second, the committee chose to adopt for its common usage the following terminology: "parish director" is the person to whom a participation in the pastoral care of the parish is entrusted; "priest supervisor" refers to the priest whom the bishop designates to supervise the pastoral care. Given the diversity of terms being used in this country, this decision is not without its drawbacks. Each of the various titles utilized (e.g., parish life coordinator, parochial minister, parish coordinator; priest moderator, parish moderator) has reasons to recommend and not to recommend adoption. Consultation with those who have had experience in the implementation of canon 517, §2 did not result in any overwhelming consensus. Some titles in usage (e.g., lay pastor and canonical pastor) were studied by the committee and found to be canonically imprecise or inaccurate.

Third, the committee opted to provide the broadest scope possible in considering areas which could be entrusted to the parish director. This decision was made mindful that local circumstances will always direct the discretion and judgement of the bishop in determining the needs of his particular church.

Fourth, although some diocesan structures or practices designate a priest or priests, separate from the priest supervisor, to provide sacramental ministry when a parish director is appointed, this model of ministry was not adopted by the committee. Minimizing the number of persons relating in a formal way to parishioners was accepted as an advantage. In those dioceses where this additional sacramental minister is appointed, additional norms and position descriptions will be needed.[3]

When a diocese is arriving at a determination to implement

3. Sample materials have been included in the Appendices for consideration when a priest is designated for this type of sacramental ministry.

canon 517, §2, there must be clarity about the nature of this canonical provision. In some instances dioceses cite canon 517, §2 as the operative norm in their attempt to provide alternate means of providing pastoral care. In effect, however, they are operating out of the provisions of either canon 517, §1 (the entrusting of the pastoral care of a parish or group of parishes to a team of priests *in solidum* with one of them designated as the moderator) or canon 526, §1 (the appointment of a priest to serve as the pastor of more than one parish). It would seem that the characteristics that would distinguish implementation of canon 517, §2 from these other provisions is the role of the priest in relation to the pastoral care of the parish. In these other instances lay persons are often assigned significant pastoral roles and responsibilities but with little effective authority with regard to decision making or administration.

In the first case, what is popularly called a "team ministry," the pastoral care of the parish or group of parishes is carried out as a common responsibility of a group of priests. One of these priests serves as a coordinator of activities and liaison to the diocesan church. A scarcity of priests is not stated as a condition for the utilization of this pastoral provision. The circumstances warranting such a pastoral provision are not stated in the canon. A dearth of priests is not stated in the canon as the rationale for the implementation of this pastoral provision. Other staff persons may be contributing significantly to the pastoral care provided but would not be doing so under the provisions of canon 517, §2.

In the second case, the implementation of canon 526, the appointment of a priest to serve as pastor of more than one parish is noted as having its origins in the dearth of priests and is thus similar in nature to the provision of canon 517, §2. The difference, however, appears to be in the very appointment of a pastor. Canon 517, §2 would seem to arise out of a situation in which there is no appointment of a pastor because of the scarcity of priests in general as well as the unavailability of priests endowed with the qualities and characteristics that are required in a pastor.

Canon 526 would seem to apply in those cases where there is a shortage of priests but it is deemed possible for an individual priest to fulfill his pastoral responsibilities in more than one parish, perhaps because of the nature, size or geographical proximity of the parishes. In fulfilling these responsibilities he may indeed rely on the services of one or more lay persons to provide pastoral care in specified areas.

In the end, and with future canonical study, the relationship between cc. 517, §2 and 526 may be clarified and they may be considered correlative canons. At this moment, however, there is reason to believe that they are distinct and this project will proceed with its analysis of canon 517, §2 as separate from canon 526. It would behoove dioceses that believe they have implemented canon 517, §2, however, to review their actual practices and underlying rationales to determine which canon they have, in effect, implemented.

In deciding to compile these materials into a handbook, it is the hope of this committee that its contents will be useful to dioceses who are already implementing this new model of parish life as they evaluate future directions as well as to those who are just beginning to venture into this area.

BARBARA ANNE CUSACK

I. *Position Descriptions*

THERESE GUERIN SULLIVAN, S.P.

Parish Director

In the absence of a pastor, canon 517, §2 recognizes the possibility that women and men who are not ordained may be entrusted with a participation in the pastoral care of a parish. The definitions given here are intended to assist those responsible to formulate role descriptions in particular circumstances. To distinguish specific areas of responsibility, the following generic definitions are provided:

Basic Definition

The parish director is a woman or man to whom a participation in the exercise of the pastoral care of a parish is entrusted. This care includes the following areas: education and pastoral services, worship, administration (cc. 517, §2; 528–537).

Role in General

The parish director should demonstrate the ability to serve in the following areas:

a. Teaching office: In the area of leadership the parish director must be able to relate aspects of parish life to the life and mission of the universal Church; to call all parishioners to service as

Church and to facilitate lay ministry and leadership in a spirit of collaboration and subsidiarity. It will also be necessary to provide educational programs and training to enable parishioners to fulfill their ministry in the Church and in the world more effectively.

b. Sanctifying office: In accord with the norms of liturgical law a parish director should strive to insure opportunities for the priest to know the people; to provide for and coordinate the celebrations of the Eucharist and other sacraments by the priests and the diocesan bishop; to participate in sacramental celebration.

c. Administration functions: In accord with diocesan policy the parish director makes provision for:

1. the preparation of persons for the celebration of the sacraments of baptism, confirmation, Eucharist, penance, anointing of the sick, and marriage;
2. the religious education of all parishioners, including youth, adults, the handicapped and the infirm;
3. the utilization of the resources offered by the diocesan religious education offices;
4. the training of religious education teachers for each of the sacraments mentioned above, and the proper implementation of the Order of Christian Initiation of Adults;
5. the assessment of needs and planning for pastoral care both directly and by way of educational programs and training for other ministers of pastoral care in areas such as ministry to the following: families, the sick, the dying, and those with special needs, for example: the handicapped, the mentally ill, the elderly, youth, the widowed, divorced and separated, the alcoholic and drug dependent, the imprisoned, those in crisis, and the disadvantaged, as well as extended parish activities in the areas of evangelization, social justice, ecumenism and participation in diocesan workshops and events.

Canonical Implications

The parish director is understood to be responsible for the administration of the parish entrusted to her/his care, under the supervision of the priest supervisor, in accord with diocesan norms. The parish director should be an ex-officio member of the parish council and the parish finance council and could be designated to preside over both councils. The parish director should be empowered to carry out all ordinary acts of administration. The diocesan norms for performing extraordinary acts of administration should be followed. Decisions regarding acts of administration should be made in concert with the priest supervisor (see Chapter 2 for canonical argumentation).

Relationship to Priest Supervisor

The parish director exercises the ministry of pastoral care of the parish under the supervision of the priest supervisor. Essential for collaboration in the exercise of these roles is a desire for good communication and an openness to work together. The parish director ought to strive to keep the priest supervisor aware of on going assessments of parish life. The assumptions, goals, time lines, and schedules of activities will assist the priest supervisor to understand planning and decisions. The parish director should inform the priest supervisor of particular situations or incidents for which he may be expected to give account. Such events might include: developing trends in pastoral need, unusual circumstances which require particular understanding or awareness, damage to church property.

Areas of Responsibility

Specific areas of responsibility entrusted to the parish director include:

a. Teaching office: In the area of education the parish director:

1. provides appropriate coordination of the sacramental cate-

chesis programs such as: pre-baptismal instruction of parents, first communion, first penance, confirmation preparation, marriage preparation (c. 528, §1);

2. maintains a spiritual and educational vision for religious education activities and or school activities in the parish;

3. promotes the role of laity and provides for an adult education ministry (c. 529, §2);

4. assures that a ministry of evangelization and outreach occurs within the parish.

b. Sanctifying office: In the area of worship the parish director:

1. administers baptism when no priest is available (cc. 230, §3; 861, §3);

2. recruits and schedules liturgical ministers (acolytes, servers, ushers, lectors, eucharistic ministers, presiders);

3. coordinates and supervises liturgical ministers;

4. provides spiritual and liturgical direction for the liturgy committee;

5. serves as extraordinary minister of the Eucharist and Viaticum (cc. 910, §2; 911, §2);

6. preaches when pastorally and canonically appropriate;

7. administers approved sacramentals (c. 1168);

8. imparts blessings designated in the ritual for blessings;

9. shares in planning and evaluation of Sunday liturgies, children's and other special group or home liturgies, seasonal liturgies and communal penance services;

10. participates in the planning and coordination of the communal Rite of Anointing;

11. promotes marriage and family life, works with couples in marriage preparation (prenuptial inquiry, petitions for matrimonial dispensations, premarital inventory);

12. assists in ministry to divorced and remarried persons and assures that access to a marriage tribunal is facilitated;

13. provides counseling and spiritual/psychological support to individuals and families;

14. assists families with funeral arrangements;
15. presides at wake services and celebrates Liturgy of the Word and Final Commendation according to the Order of Christian Funerals;
16. plans and coordinates the Order of Christian Initiation of Adults;
17. presides at weekday liturgy (liturgy of the hours and Communion service or liturgy of the word and Communion service) and on Sundays (liturgy of the word and Communion service), subject to regulations of the Code of Canon Law and diocesan norms;
18. oversees sacramental life of the parish.

c. Administrative functions: In the area of administration the parish director:

1. reports to the priest supervisor regularly on all facets of the life of the parish;
2. represents the parish community (practically, even if not juridically) and is involved in ecumenical, area, cluster, deanery, vicariate and diocesan networks of pastors (even though she/he is not canonically the same as a pastor);
3. establishes structures for collaborative functioning and shared decision-making such as the parish council, finance council, town hall meetings (cc. 535; 537);
4. maintains parish sacramental records, death records, parish archives and prepares annual reports requested by the diocese (c.535);
5. administers the material assets of the parish, oversees maintenance of buildings, finances, fund-raising, and budget preparation in accordance with particular law and in collaboration with the finance council (cc. 535; 537);
6. invites the parish community to articulate its mission/vision in the light of the Gospel and promulgates it;
7. discerns parish needs and plans for the future in collaboration with the priest supervisor and parish leaders to ensure effective parish programs related to real needs;

8. ensures that there is ongoing evaluation of parish life, programs and staff functioning in the context of the mission/vision;
9. selects staff members capable of performing ministries in response to parish needs, vision, and mission;
10. oversees the formation, training, and ongoing development of the staff, encouraging freedom and creativity;
11. forms a faith community among staff members, supporting and affirming them;
12. provides opportunities for prayer and celebration with staff.

Priest Supervisor

Basic Definition

The priest supervisor provides supervision of the pastoral care given by the parish director. He is accountable to the bishop and collaborates with the parish director. He provides the sacraments in a parish where there is a parish director. In cases where the priest supervisor is the priest who supplies regular Sunday help to the parish, or is assigned to a neighboring parish, a clear delineation of roles should be made at the time of the appointment.

Role in General

The priest supervisor should have a deep understanding of the nature of collaborative ministry. It is essential that he understand the baptismal call of every Christian to ministry and be solidly rooted in Vatican II theology and liturgical reform. Therefore the priest supervisor must demonstrate a pastoral ability to:

a. accept the role of the parish director and support and assist her/him in that role;
b. afford the laity their rightful place in liturgical celebrations;
c. serve as spiritual advisor;
d. provide pastoral counseling on request;

e. communicate with others;

f. deal with conflict.

The priest supervisor is to provide a mentoring role from his own experience. Because of possible confusion of roles it would be advisable that the priest supervisor not have been a pastor or associate pastor of the parish now being served by the parish director.

Canonical Implications

The priest supervisor is appointed by the diocesan bishop to supervise the pastoral care of the parish. Therefore, the priest supervisor could be the dean, another local priest, or a priest member of the diocesan curia.

The priest supervisor enjoys all the powers and faculties of pastor including the ordinary faculty to officiate at marriages in accordance with the norms of canon 1110. He is not the canonical equivalent of a pastor and, while he has the powers and faculties of a pastor he does not assume the canonical rights and obligations of a pastor. Any *ipso iure* faculties which general or particular law concedes to a pastor, would automatically be conferred upon the supervising priest at the time of his appointment.

It is understood that the priest supervisor would devote some care and attention to the parish entrusted to the care of the parish director and visit said parish as often as conveniently possible to insure that all of the pastoral responsibilities are fulfilled.

The term of office is determined by the diocesan bishop and is not limited to the six year tenure but is for an indefinite or definite period of time to be determined by the diocesan bishop (c. 522).

Relationship to Parish Director

The priest supervisor is appointed to supervise the pastoral care of the parish assigned to a parish director. For this reason, the priest supervisor ought to seek to be informed of the parish life, its needs, growth and development, as well as how the parish director is responding to pastoral need. Mutual trust, and respect will contribute to genuine collaboration. It is essential that the priest supervisor and the parish director communicate regularly to increase, enhance and foster mutual understanding.

Areas of Responsibility

The areas of responsibility assigned to the priest supervisor need to be delineated in writing at the time of his appointment by the bishop in accordance with the norm of law (c. 517, §2). These areas of responsibility include:

a. Teaching office: In addition to exercising the power and faculties of a pastor, (c. 517, §2), the priest supervisor's duties may include being available for information, advice, clarification and mutual support when needed.

b. Sanctifying office: Responsibilities may include the obligation of celebrating the Mass for the people (c. 534) and the faculty to administer confirmation in the following circumstances: to those in danger of death (c. 883, §3); to adult non-Catholics, including all who are no longer infants, who are being received into full communion, in the rite of their admission; to those returning to the Church, in the Order of Christian Initiation when other adults are being received into communion.

c. Administrative functions: The priest supervisor should:

1. be knowledgeable of the diocese, deanery, and the local area under his supervision;
2. assist in planning for and evaluate the effectiveness of parish ministry;
3. see to it that sufficient understanding of roles exists.

Qualifications/Eligibility of the Parish Director

The search for suitable candidates to fill the role of parish director in a particular parish ought to be based on a needs assessment of the parish. A variety of desired qualities and skills, demonstrated in academic achievement and established in ministerial experience should be used in the selection process. The selection process should evaluate:

Professional Qualifications

a. *Priority* should be given applicants who have:

1. a master's degree in pastoral ministry, theology, scripture, liturgy, or a closely related field of religious study;
2. experience of three or more years in some phase of parish ministry (e.g., sacramental preparation, RCIA, catechesis, liturgy, spiritual direction, counseling);
3. at least one year working in the diocese;
4. background in sacramental rites, liturgy of the word and communion services, prayer, homiletics, canon law, tribunal processes, administration, team ministry, budgeting and finance.

b. *Consideration* may also be given applicants who have:

1. a bachelor's degree in a field related to parish ministry;
2. experience of three or more years in some phase of parish ministry;
3. background in aspects of pastoral administration and a willingness to augment their basic education and to develop new skills.

c. *By way of exception:*

1. educationally qualified applicants who lack practical experience may be asked to complete a one year supervised internship with appropriate remuneration as a prerequisite to official appointment by the bishop;
2. promising applicants who lack necessary educational requirements may be accepted on a probationary basis provided they undertake a college level program (e.g., an institute for pastoral life, etc.) financed by the diocese and judged by the diocese to include areas of ministry essential to the ministry of the pastoral administrator;

3. formal appointment by the bishop follows successful completion of the internship or studies program provided for through written agreement between the diocese and the applicant.

Personal Qualifications to be Considered

a. general good health (physical, psychological, spiritual);

b. liturgically based spirituality centered on the prayer life of the Church;

c. experience maintaining confidentiality;

d. skill as initiator; ability to organize, to work in collaboration, to facilitate, to delegate;

e. reasonable familiarity with the area, people, culture;

f. commitment to personal and professional growth.

Accountability/Evaluation of the Parish Director

Accountability

The parish director is ultimately accountable to the diocesan bishop. The parish director is immediately accountable to the priest supervisor with whom he/she meets regularly for the purposes of self-evaluation and sharing of information regarding:

a. the parish and its missions if any;

b. on-going communication between and among the parish director, the priest supervisor and the bishop for the harmonious exercise of their respective ministry roles.

As with any ministry position, it is presumed the parish director recognizes responsibility toward the faith community in which she/he ministers as a primary form of accountability.

Evaluation

The evaluation of the parish director should be based on performance in such areas as:

a. Diocesan level: The parish director is to:

1. be familiar with diocesan policies, handbooks and procedures;
2. demonstrate support for the mission statement of the diocese;
3. promote the implementation of its pastoral plan;
4. abide by diocesan guidelines and policies in all that pertains to parish pastoral administration;
5. receive all diocesan communications that pertain to the position of parish director, and to be consulted regarding decisions affecting her/his ministry or the life of the parish;
6. submit reports, respecting deadlines established by the diocese. In addition, the parish director is to attend and participate in meetings concerning pastoral leadership and parishes.

b. Parish level: The parish director is to:

1. collaborate with the priest supervisor for the coordination and directing of parish liturgy;
2. facilitate clear, honest and open communication within the parish and between the parish and the diocese, its offices and staffs;
3. exercise ministry in a spirit of collaboration and subsidiarity;
4. relate aspects of parish life to the life and mission of the universal church to strengthen bonds of unity with the broader community of faith, its joys, pains and needs;
5. initiate and provide for ecumenical involvement wherever possible;
6. involve parishioners in the administrative function of the parish;
7. familiarize the pastoral council and the finance council with their respective administrative roles and evaluate their performance;
8. keep accurate records, particularly insofar as these reflect the sacramental of the parish;

9. preside at meetings within the parish as required;
10. exercise stewardship over parish properties, and help to foster a sense of stewardship (development and divestment) within the parish;
11. keep books and prepare budgets in collaboration with pastoral councils and volunteers in ways consistent with their respective roles;
12. oversee all parish maintenance, repairs and construction.

II. *Special Authorizations or Faculties*

BARBARA ANNE CUSACK

General Principles

A faculty is an empowerment to act granted by a competent authority to one who otherwise does not have the authority to act. While the law itself grants some faculties[1], others are conceded by means of an administrative act by which the competent authority grants a favor. Within a diocese, certain faculties are granted by the diocesan bishop. He may do so himself or may delegate another to grant them in his name.

Because of the unresolved issues on the relationship between governance and orders, there has been some hesitation to speak of the granting of "faculties" to lay persons. This current project does not set out to resolve these theological and canonical issues. Therefore, we will not use the term "faculties" when referring to special authorization to be given to lay parish directors. Many of the same principles relating to faculties, their grant, restriction, removal, should be taken into account, however, when lay parish directors are to be authorized for special functions within the parish.

1. For a list of such *ipso iure* faculties granted to clerics, see James Provost, "Faculties," in *Clergy Procedural Handbook* (Washington: Canon Law Society of America, 1992) 104–106.

Since the issuance of faculties or the grant of special authorization is an administrative act, the general norms on administrative acts should be followed. Thus the appropriate factual information about the candidate should be obtained (c. 50) and the faculties should be issued in writing (c. 51). Likewise, the restriction or revocation of faculties or authorization also needs to follow the norms on administrative acts (c. 58).

In making determinations about what authorizations should be issued to parish directors and faculties to priest supervisors, the diocesan bishop should have as his primary concern the pastoral care of the parish to which these ministers will be appointed. There would be great latitude regarding what could be granted. An examination of the basic mission of the Church as lived out within this particular faith community would precede any decisions about the grant of faculties or authorizations. The teaching, sanctifying and governing mission of the Church would be the basic context for consideration of appropriate faculties or authorizations to be granted.

In some instances the empowerment or capacity to act in relation to the particular community of the Christian faithful demands certain prerequisites among which is presbyteral orders. For example, the priest supervisor may be granted the faculty to confirm already baptized Catholics but a lay (or deacon) parish director cannot be so authorized.

Parish Director

Authorizations which could be granted to a parish director can be categorized into the various areas of ministry or the three *munera* of the Church. The pastoral care to be offered within the parish setting would fall within these areas and therefore would provide the areas for "participation in pastoral care" to be exercised by the parish director. Determinations about what parish directors would be authorized to do would be guided by both the needs of the parish and the qualifications of the parish director.

For example, authorization to preach at daily Communion services or at Sunday worship in the absence of a priest would require that the parish director be adequately prepared by means of preaching courses and practical experience.

Teaching Office

Canon 528, §1 describes the exercise of the teaching office of the pastor. By analogy this canon may surface some of the various teaching functions which would be undertaken by a parish director in the absence of a pastor. Some of these functions may be assigned to the parish director.

The major teaching office responsibilities of the pastor stated in canon 528, §1 are as follows:

a. to see that the Word of God in its entirety is announced to those living in the parish;

b. to see that parishioners are instructed in Christian doctrine;

c. to preach homilies;

d. to provide catechetical formation;

e. to foster works in the spirit of the Gospel including works of social justice;

f. to take special care for the Catholic education of children and young adults;

g. to evangelize among those who are not practicing their faith or do not profess the faith.

Among these areas of responsibility there is only one which would not be able to be fulfilled by the lay parish director: the preaching of the homily is reserved to a priest or deacon (c. 767). However, other forms of preaching can be undertaken by the lay parish director. Canon 766 provides the criteria under which lay persons may be admitted to preach in a church or oratory: necessity and utility. Preaching by lay persons is to be exercised in accord with the norms issued by the conference of bishops and, if applicable, those of the diocesan bishop, the moderator of preaching in the particular church (c. 772).

Since the preaching of the word of God is an important element in the faith development of the community, in the absence of an ordained minister with the faculty to preach, it would seem necessary that an appropriate lay person, in this case the parish director, be authorized to preach. In addition, in those settings in which both the lay parish director and the priest supervisor are present, for example at a funeral, it may be more useful for the parish director to assume the preaching responsibility based on his or her understanding of and relationship to the family or deceased.

Given these factors, the diocesan bishop should consider the granting of authorization to preach the word of God to qualified lay parish directors. The exercise of this preaching function, as with all of the ministry performed, would be under the moderation of the priest supervisor. In those instances in which the priest supervisor or another ordained minister will be present, it would be important that advance planning and coordination take place so that the appropriate person preaches on the given occasion.

Pastoral responsibility for and leadership in the teaching mission of the Church at the parish level are described elsewhere in the code. The pastor's responsibilities for the ministry of the word including preaching, catechetical ministry, education and sacramental preparation are described in canons 757; 767; 770; 771; 773; 776; 777; 794, §2; 851, 2°; 890; 914; 1001 and 1063. Among those responsibilities are the following:

a. to proclaim the Gospel especially through the ministry of preaching exercised both personally and through others as in the case of overseeing the preaching of homilies, arranging for parish retreats or missions, and through evangelization;

b. to provide for catechesis of the faithful with catechetical formation of adults, young people, and children;

c. to foster the role of parents in family catechesis;

d. to see that appropriate sacramental preparation is provided;

e. to make provision for catechetical formation for those with special needs.

With the exception of the preaching of the homily, none of these prescribed responsibilities of the pastor require the exercise of sacred orders. Therefore, the parish director could be authorized to fulfill these responsibilities in those parishes in which a pastor is not present. The absence of a pastor would appear to constitute a situation of necessity as well as one in which a sacred minister is lacking as indicated in canon 230, §3. In such a situation a lay person may "exercise the ministry of the word." Again, with the exception of preaching, those elements which would constitute this exercise of the ministry of the word would more appropriately be stated in the position description than in the designation of special "authorization."

Sanctifying Office

Canon 230, §3 also indicates ministries within the sanctifying office of the Church which lay persons may exercise under the same conditions of necessity and lack of sacred ministers. These ministries are listed as:

a. presiding over liturgical prayers;
b. conferring baptism;
c. distributing Holy Communion.

The exercise of the sanctifying office by a pastor is described in summary fashion in canons 528, §2 and 530. Among the responsibilities of the pastor found there are the following:

a. seeing that the Eucharist is the center of the parish assembly and that the faithful knowingly and actively participate in the liturgy and devoutly receive the sacraments, especially Eucharist and penance;

b. presiding over the Eucharist on Sundays and holy days of obligation;

c. promoting personal and family prayer;

d. administering the sacraments of baptism, confirmation in danger of death, Viaticum and the anointing of the sick;

e. assisting at marriages and bestowing the nuptial blessing;

f. performing of funerals;

g. blessing of the baptismal font, leading processions and imparting solemn blessings outside the church.

These general descriptions of the exercise of the sanctifying office by the pastor are detailed elsewhere in the code especially in Book IV. It is the pastor who presides over the baptismal ministry within the parish (c. 862), confirms catechumens, those received into full communion, and those in danger of death (c. 883, 2° and 3°), provides for preparation and reception of first Eucharist and penance (c. 914), celebrates the sacrament of penance by being available to parishioners and providing opportunities for individual confession (c. 986, §1), administers the sacrament of the anointing of the sick to his parishioners (c. 1003, §2), officiates at or delegates another to officiate at marriages within his parish (cc. 1108; 1109; 1111).

Numerous pastoral responsibilities require the exercise of sacred orders. Thus a parish director could not be authorized for such responsibilities as the celebration of Eucharist, confirmation, penance, or anointing of the sick. The parish director could be responsible for the preparation in relation to these sacraments as well as the administrative details related to them, as will be seen below.

It would be possible, however, for the diocesan bishop to designate some areas of sacramental ministry to the parish director. Given the unique circumstances of each parish setting, the bishop would need to determine whether or not he would depute the lay parish director to baptize (c. 861, §2), to serve as an extraordinary minister of the Eucharist and Viaticum (cc. 910, §2; 911, §2), to serve as a minister of Eucharistic exposition and reposition (c. 943), to assist at marriage (c. 1112), to administer sacramentals (c. 1168). Liturgical norms would allow for the lay parish director to be authorized to preside at certain parts of Christian funerals such as the vigil, the rite of committal, the funeral liturgy outside of Mass.[2] Consideration will also need to be given, based on the unique conditions of each diocese, to the role of the lay parish director in Sunday celebrations in the absence of a priest.[3] Liturgical norms regarding the sacraments of initiation will need to be taken into account if the parish director is deputed to baptize. Since the norms call for the integrity of the sacraments of baptism, confirmation and Eucharist when the one being baptized is of "catechetical age," it would seem that authorization for baptism would apply only to those who have not yet reached the age of reason, generally accepted as seven years of age.[4]

The parish director would need no special authorization to exercise some facets of the Church's sanctifying mission such as presiding at the liturgy of the hours, distributing blessed ashes, imparting those blessings designated in the Book of Blessings.

Administrative Functions

The administrative responsibilities assigned by law to the pastor are many and varied. They include such activities as visiting and caring for parishioners in all of their diversity (c. 529, §1), presiding over the parish pastoral council and the parish finance council (cc. 536; 537), maintaining the parish sacramental and death registers and the parish archives (c. 535). Since the pastor represents the parish in all juridic affairs (c. 532) he is bound to the obligations of an administrator (cc. 1279–1288). It is the pas-

2. See *The Order of Christian Funerals,* nn. 14, 182, 275. It should be noted, however, that in the November 1990 plenary assembly of the National Conference of Catholic Bishops the request that diocesan bishops be authorized to permit lay persons to preside at the Funeral Liturgy outside of Mass (cf. *Ordo Exsequiarium,* 1969, nn. 19 and 22:4) failed to receive approval by the required two thirds majority vote. Therefore, at the time of this writing, this portion of the ritual book, *The Order of Christian Funerals,* approved by the NCCB in November 1985 (which approval was confirmed by the Congregation for Divine Worship in April 1987), is not yet to be implemented.

3. See, *Gathered in Steadfast Faith: Statement on Sunday Worship in the Absence of a Priest* (Washington: USCC, 1991).

4. See *Rite of Christian Initiation of Adults,* n. 344 (Chicago: Liturgy Training Publications, 1988).

tor who maintains the records related to Mass offerings and intentions (c. 958). Under prescribed conditions in danger of death or when all is prepared, the pastor may grant dispensations from certain matrimonial impediments (cc. 1079; 1080); to dispense is a formal administrative act. The granting of certain permissions (cc. 862; 1115) may also be considered as administrative functions of the pastor.

In addition to these administrative responsibilities designated by law, others may be delegated to the pastor by the diocesan bishop or local ordinary. The granting of marriage permissions or dispensations under ordinary circumstances may be delegated to the pastor.

Since none of these actions explicitly requires the exercise of sacred orders, at first glance it would appear that the parish director could be authorized to fulfill any or all of these administrative functions. The parish director would do so by means of delegated authority granted by the diocesan bishop. The delegation could be granted to the parish director at the time of appointment.

All these administrative functions do not entail acts of governance. Therefore, any concerns about the application of canon 129, §2 would not be relevant. In those instances where the administrative activity would involve the exercise of the power of governance, such as in the granting of marriage dispensations, it would be at the discretion of the diocesan bishop whether or not the circumstances warrant a delegation which would entail a cooperation in his exercise of the power of governance as envisioned in canon 129, §2.[5]

The two areas of administration that may need further examination are the delegation to represent the parish in all juridic affairs and the presiding over the pastoral and finance councils. There is some disagreement among commentators whether these functions could be delegated to the parish director or are to be

5. It must be observed that there remain varying opinions on the application of canon 129, §2 to the delegation of the power to dispense. It is not the purpose of this present study to resolve such issues.

fulfilled by law by the priest supervisor. Those who maintain that the priest supervisor is to fulfill these roles base their position on the interpretation that the phrase "endowed with the powers and faculties of a pastor" (c. 517, §2) is equivalent to "the power to act as pastor."[6] Others maintain that, in the process of revision leading to canon 517, §2, the decision of the Code Commission to delete the phrase "as the proper pastor of the parish"[7] is significant in interpreting the text. The priest supervisor is not canonically equivalent to a pastor or he would be so designated. He is said to have the "powers and faculties" of a pastor. Are juridic representation and presiding over the pastoral and finance councils either powers or faculties? If they are interpreted to be such, then obviously the priest supervisor fulfills these administrative functions. If these functions are not interpreted as powers or faculties but rather as administrative responsibilities, could they not be part of the responsibilities the parish director is delegated to fulfill?

Regardless of the conclusion reached on this issue, with regard to the question of juridic representation, the parish director could be appointed to administer the property of the parish in accord with the norm of canon 1279, §2. This canon notes that when a public juridic person does not have an administrator by law, the ordinary to whom the juridic person is subject is to appoint a suitable person as administrator. A parish is a juridic person by the law itself (c. 515, §3). According to canon 532 it is the pastor who is ordinarily the administrator of the goods of the parish as a juridic person. However, when a parish is cared for under the provisions of canon 517, §2, there is no pastor, hence no ordinary administrator. Therefore, as the ordinary to whom the parish is subject, the diocesan bishop could appoint the parish director as the administrator of the property of the parish. The parish director would observe the requirements of canons 1281–1288 in fulfilling this role.

6. See John Renken, "Canonical Issues in the Pastoral Care of Parishes Without Pastors," *The Jurist* 47 (1987) 516.

7. *Communicationes* 13 (1981) 149.

Likewise, separable from definitive resolutions of the theoretical questions surrounding the relationship between the role of a pastor and that of a priest supervisor, the diocesan bishop could designate the parish director to preside over the advisory councils of the parish. Such an appointment may be viewed as pastorally appropriate given the broad range of responsibilities assumed by the parish director.

Since the parish pastoral council has as its major function to provide assistance in fostering the pastoral activity of the parish (c. 536, §1), and since participation in the exercise of the pastoral care of the parish is entrusted to the parish director, he or she would appear to be the appropriate person to preside over this council. Given what has been said above regarding the parish director as the administrator of the property of the parish, it would also appear appropriate that he or she select and preside over the finance council of the parish according to established diocesan norms (c. 537).

Neither of these two provisions would exclude the participation of the priest supervisor in the meetings of these two councils. However, the respective roles of the parish director and the priest supervisor should be clearly delineated and mutually respected lest any divisive factors or conflicts be generated within these groups.

Priest Supervisor

Canon 517, §2 specifically states that the priest supervisor is endowed with the powers and faculties of a pastor. Therefore, any *ipso iure* faculties which general or particular law concedes to a pastor would automatically be conferred upon the priest who is appointed to supervise pastoral care when a parish director has been assigned to a parish. In addition to the faculties attached to the office of pastor, the diocesan bishop may elect to grant other faculties to the priest supervisor based on his judgement that such faculties will facilitate the pastoral care being provided by the priest supervisor.

Ipso Iure *Faculties*

Canon law requires that, in addition to presbyteral orders, the minister of the sacrament of penance also possess the faculty to hear confessions (c. 966, §1). The law itself grants this faculty, by reason of office, to "the pastor of a parish and those who take the place of the pastor of a parish" (c. 968, §1). The priest supervisor, who is by law "endowed with the powers and faculties of a pastor," enjoys this required faculty. Once he possesses this faculty by reason of office, he can exercise it not only within the confines of the parish to which he is assigned as supervisor, but also anywhere else unless in a particular case a local ordinary prohibits such an exercise (c. 967, §2).

A faculty is also required for a priest or deacon to preach. However, the law itself grants such a faculty and allows for its universal exercise, with at least the presumed consent of the rector of the church, and unless an ordinary removes the faculty or places a restriction on its exercise, or particular law requires explicit permission for its exercise (c. 764). Hence, under ordinary circumstances a priest supervisor would not need an additional grant of a faculty to preach.

According to canon 1108, §1 the form for marriage, in which at least one party is Catholic, requires the presence of a local ordinary, a pastor, or a priest or deacon properly delegated by either of them. Canon 1109 further states that, barring excommunication, interdict or suspension from office, a local ordinary and pastor validly assist by reason of office at marriages within the confines of the territory of the parish. Because he is endowed with the powers and faculties of a pastor, the priest supervisor would validly assist at marriages celebrated within the parish to which he is assigned. Likewise, as long as he holds this office, he can delegate other priests or deacons this same faculty to assist at marriages within the parish (c. 1111, §1).

The delegation of a priest or deacon for marriage would become a particular issue of concern in those situations in which the priest supervisor is not the priest who is responsible for the regular sacramental care of the parish. In such a case, the priest supervisor would need to grant delegation of the faculty to a specified priest or deacon and, if it is a matter of special delegation, for a specific marriage; if general delegation for all marriages celebrated within the parish is to be granted, it is to be in writing to the specified priest or deacon (c. 1111, §2).

Additional Faculties

Aside from those faculties which are granted by law or office, the diocesan bishop may deem it appropriate to confer on the priest supervisor additional faculties in order to provide for the needs of the parish community. Many dioceses have a standard *pagella* of faculties issued to priests within the diocese. Any of those faculties which are applicable to pastors would also be granted automatically to priest supervisors. Other additional faculties may be granted to all priests and would likewise be applicable to the priest supervisor.[8]

8. A sample list of faculties frequently included in a diocesan *pagella* is included in Appendix C to this section.

Appendix A

Sample List of Authorizations for Parish Director

By the power invested in me as diocesan bishop, I entrust to you the following functions in order to foster your ministry as parish director. This authorization remains in effect until revocation, for whatever reason, or until your appointment as parish director ceases. These functions are to be exercised only within the parish to which you are appointed.

(The granting of any or all of these functions remains at the prudential discretion of the diocesan bishop depending upon need or usefulness as exist within the given diocese and parish.)

Preaching

To preach the word of God (c. 766) at (any or all of the following settings could be designated)

* daily Communion service or Liturgy of the Word;
* Sunday service (when no priest is available for Celebration of the Eucharist);
* funeral vigil, wake service, committal service, funeral liturgy;
* Liturgy of the Hours;
* baptism.

Sacramental and Liturgical Ministry

To baptize children under the age of seven according to the approved rituals (c. 861, §2; *Rite of Baptism*);

To serve as an extraordinary minister of the Eucharist and Viaticum (c. 910, §2; 911, §2);

To serve as a minister of Eucharistic exposition and reposition (c. 943);

To assist at marriage (c. 1112);

To administer sacramentals such as blessed ashes on Ash Wednesday, blessing of throats on the Feast of St. Blase, blessing of a communicant (c. 1168);

To present to the local ordinary names of those to be designated liturgical ministers (c. 230, §3).

Administration

To serve as representative of the parish in juridic affairs (c. 532);

To preside over parish pastoral and finance councils in accord with diocesan norms (cc. 536; 537);

To maintain parish sacramental records and issue authentic sacramental documents (c. 535, §§1-3);

To preserve and maintain parish archives (c. 535, §§4, 5);

To serve as administrator of parish property (cc. 1281–1288).

Given at _____

Date _____

_____   _____
Bishop   Notary

(Seal)

Appendix B

Letter Withdrawing Authorization

Parish Director

Parish

Dear *(Parish Director)*,

Having investigated and reviewed the pastoral situation at *(Parish)* and having discussed this matter with you, by means of this letter I am notifying you that [the following functions: (list those to be withdrawn) OR all special authorization] previously granted to you in your role as parish director are withdrawn as of this date.

Sincerely,

Bishop	Notary

Date _____

Place _____

(Seal)

Appendix C

Sample List of Faculties for Priest Supervisor

In accord with canon 517, §2, as a validly appointed priest supervisor, you enjoy and may exercise within the confines of the parish to which you are assigned, all of the powers and faculties of a pastor granted by universal law. Those *ipso iure* faculties are as follows:

To confirm those who have attained the use of reason and whom they baptize or receive into full communion (c. 883, 2°);

To hear confessions (granted as an habitual faculty) (c. 968, §1);

To grant dispensations from prescribed marriage impediments in danger of death (c. 1079, §2) or when everything is *omnia parata* (c. 1080) in accord with the norm of law;

To assist at marriages celebrated within the boundaries of the parish to which one is assigned and to delegate other priests and deacons to assist at such marriages (cc. 1108; 1109; 1111);

To permit the celebration of the marriage of a Catholic in a Catholic church or oratory other than the proper parish church (c. 1115; 1118, §1);

To dispense, in individual cases and for a just cause, from the obligation to observe a holyday or day of penance, or to commute the obligation to some other pious work (c. 1245);

To dispense from private vows, to commute the obligation arising from a private vow; to suspend, dispense, or commute a promissory oath (cc. 1196, 1°; 1197; 1203).

In order to facilitate the ministry you will perform, I also grant you the following faculties. These faculties are to be exercised only within the parish(es) to which you are appointed.

(The granting of any or all of these faculties remains at the prudential discretion of the diocesan bishop depending upon need or usefulness as exist within the given diocese and parish. However, any faculties which are granted by particular law to pastors are also granted to priest supervisors.)

To baptize persons who have reached the age of 14 without referring the matter to the diocesan bishop (c. 863);

To confirm those who were baptized but never raised as Catholic at the time they are returning to the Church (c. 883, §1);

To celebrate the Eucharist, for good reason, twice on weekdays and, as pastoral need requires, three times on Sundays and holydays of obligation (c. 905, §2);

To remit, without the necessity of recourse, in the internal or external forum, a *latae sententiae* penalty established by law but not yet declared provided such remission is not reserved to the Apostolic See (c. 1355, §2). (In this case the bishop may wish to delineate specific offenses, e.g., abortion, for which penalties may be remitted rather than this general grant of a faculty to remit all penalties.);

To dispense, even in cases which are not occult, all marriage impediments which the local ordinary may dispense when the need for the dispensation is discovered after everything has been prepared and the marriage cannot be delayed without probable danger of grave harm until the dispensation can be obtained from competent authority (c. 1080);

To grant permission for the celebration of the marriage of a Catholic with a person baptized in another Christian church or ecclesial communion provided the provisions of canon 1125 are fulfilled (c. 1124);

To dispense, for just and reasonable cause, from the impediment of disparity of worship provided the conditions of canon 1125 are fulfilled (c. 1086);

To dispense from the observance of the canonical form in a religiously mixed marriage if serious difficulties pose an obstacle to its observance provided the marriage will be celebrated within the diocese and there will be a public form of celebration (cc. 1127; 1129);

To permit the marriage of two Catholics or of a Catholic and a baptized non-Catholic to be celebrated in a suitable place other than a church or oratory (c. 1118, §2);

To allow church funeral rites for an unbaptized child whom the parents had intended to have baptized (c. 1183, §2);

To allow church funeral rites for a baptized non-Catholic provided such would not be contrary to the wishes of the deceased and a minister of the faith of the deceased is not available (c. 1183, §3).

Given at _____

Date _____

_____   _____
Bishop   Notary

(Seal)

Appendix D

Sacramental Minister

There may be situations in which the needs and personnel considerations of the diocese advise appointing a priest, in addition to the priest supervisor, to a parish entrusted to the care of a parish director. This additional priest will often have as his main function to provide sacramental ministry. A variety of titles have been devised for him: "sacramental minister" (because of the primary role he fulfills); "assisting priest" (because his role is seen as assisting in the pastoral care of the parish). Regardless of titles, his role should be clearly delineated and his working relationship with both the parish director and priest supervisor. Lines of authority and processes for decision-making among these three should also be clear.

Offered here is a sample description and list of responsibilities that could be used for such a priest appointment as well as a sample of faculties which could be issued to him.

Position Description

Rationale. Members of a parish under the care of a parish director retain their right to have access to the sacraments (c. 213). The diocesan bishop has a responsibility to see that the faithful have the opportunity for sacramental celebrations within the diocese (c. 387). Therefore, when a bishop appoints a parish director to a parish he may also need to appoint to the same parish, in addition to the priest supervisor, a priest who will provide the sacramental and pastoral care which require priestly ministry.

Purpose of Position. The purpose of this position is to ensure that sacramental and pastoral care which require priestly ministry are provided to a parish entrusted to a parish director. The priest who fulfills this role is understood to be assisting in the pastoral care of the parish even though he is not appointed to a full time position within the parish.

Accountability. Since both the parish director and this priest are appointed by the diocesan bishop, ultimate accountability in the fulfillment of their respective offices is to him. Since the priest supervisor is appointed specifically to supervise pastoral care, both the parish director and this priest are accountable to him for the quality of pastoral care being provided in the parish. The priest and parish director work collaboratively with one another to provide a full scope of pastoral care to parishioners. In those areas which have been designated as the responsibility of the parish director, decision making authority rests with him/her, and the priest is accountable to him/her in carrying out those decisions.

Responsibilities.

1. To preside at Eucharistic celebrations on Sundays and holy days according to the schedule mutually arranged by him and the parish director. To offer a Mass for the intention for the people of the parish (c. 534) on each Sunday and holy day (if this responsibility has not been given to the priest supervisor).

2. To celebrate other sacraments according to a schedule mutually arranged between himself and the parish director. At the time of his appointment the priest is granted general delegation to assist at all marriages within the territory of the parish (c. 1111, §1). In addition, all faculties ordinarily designated to an associate pastor are also granted to him at the time of his appointment.

3. As his schedule permits, to participate in meetings at which the planning takes place for liturgies at which he will preside. The priest will be invited to attend, as his schedule permits, parish social events and meetings in order to establish and support pastoral contacts among the people with whom he celebrates sacraments.

4. To meet regularly with the parish director mutually to assess and plan the entire scope of pastoral care being provided.

5. To meet quarterly with the priest supervisor for purposes of evaluation.

Sample of Faculties

In addition to those faculties which you already possess (e.g., to preach the Word of God), in order to facilitate the ministry you will perform at _____ Parish, I grant you the following faculties. These faculties are to be exercised only within the parish(es) to which you are appointed.

To baptize persons who have reached the age of 14 without referring the matter to the diocesan bishop (c. 863);

To administer the sacrament of confirmation to those persons who have attained the use of reason and whom you baptize (c. 883, 2°);

To confirm those persons who have attained the use of reason and are already baptized in another church or ecclesial communion when you receive such persons into full communion (c. 884, §1);

To celebrate the Eucharist, for good reason, twice on weekdays and, as pastoral need requires, three times on Sundays and holydays of obligation (c. 905, §2);

To dispense in individual cases and for just cause, from the Eucharistic fast (c. 919, §1);

To hear confessions granted as an habitual faculty (c. 968);

To remit, without the necessity of recourse, in the internal forum the *latae sententiae* penalty of excommunication (c. 1357, §2) established by law for procuring a completed abortion;

To assist at marriages within the boundaries of the parish to which you are assigned (c. 1111, §1);

To dispense, even in cases which are not occult, all marriage impediments which the local ordinary may dispense when the need for the dispensation is discovered after everything has been prepared and the marriage cannot be delayed without probable danger of grave harm until the dispensation can be obtained from competent authority (c. 1080);

To grant permission for the celebration of the marriage of a Catholic with a person baptized in another Christian church or ecclesial communion (mixed religion permission) provided the provisions of canon 1125 are fulfilled (c. 1124);

To grant permission for the celebration of the marriage of a Catholic with a Catholic who has notoriously rejected the Catholic faith provided the conditions of canon 1125 are fulfilled (c. 1071);

To permit an individual baptized non-Catholic to receive the Eucharist within his/her own marriage ceremony. This permission is not to be given unless the conditions of canon 844 are met and does not include general permission to all non-Catholics in attendance;

To dispense from private vows, to commute the obligation arising from a private vow, to suspend, dispense, or commute a promissory oath (cc. 1196; 1197; 1203);

To dispense, in individual cases and for a just cause, from the obligation to observe a holyday or day of penance, or to commute the obligation to some other pious work (c. 1245).

Any additional faculties which are granted by particular law to associate pastors are also granted to you by virtue of your role at _____ Parish.

Given at _____

Date _____

_____   _____
Bishop   Notary

(Seal)

III. *Procedures*

BARBARA ANNE CUSACK

General Principles

The Church has committed itself to standards of justice which must be reflected not only in its teaching but also in its practices. In the document *Justice in the World,* the 1971 Synod of Bishops presented the following challenge to the Church:

While the Church is bound to give witness to justice, it recognizes that anyone who ventures to speak to people about justice must first be just in their eyes. Hence we must undertake an examination of the modes of acting . . . within the Church itself. Within the Church rights must be preserved. No one should be deprived of rights because he or she is associated with the Church in one way or another. Those who serve the Church by their labor . . . should receive sufficient livelihood and enjoy that social security which is customary in their region. Lay persons should be given fair wages and a system of promotion.[1]

The bishops in the United States reiterated this principle in their pastoral letter, "Economic Justice for All: Catholic Social Teaching and the American Economy."[2] They recognized that, as

1. Synod of Bishops, *De Iustitia in Mundo,* III, November 30, 1971, in *AAS* 63 (1971) 933; English translation in ed. David Byers, *Justice in the Marketplace* (Washington: USCC, 1985) 257.

2. National Conference of Catholic Bishops, "Economic Justice for All:

an "economic actor" the Church must not only proclaim moral principles and call for justice in the work place but must also be exemplary in its own employment practices.[3]

In order to "offer directions and challenges to the institutional Church to be an employer that exemplifies and models just, equitable, and fair personnel policies,"[4] the National Association of Church Personnel Administrators has proposed principles for action in the hiring, retaining, supervising and terminating of church personnel. Among these principles we find the following:

1. that recruitment and placement of church personnel reflect fair procedures for hiring or assignment and be based on publicly stated selection procedures;
2. that fair and honest evaluation procedures occur at regular, predetermined intervals;
3. that grievance procedures and due process methods be well publicized and accessible;
4. that termination procedures include clear identification of the reasons why an employee may be terminated and that they delineate and affirm the rights and obligations of each person involved in the termination process.[5]

In an effort to respond to this challenge, each diocese should commit itself to the development of policies and procedures that protect and promote justice within the Church. Such policies and procedures are still being developed in relation to the Church's selection and appointment of, as well as the ongoing relationship with, those lay persons to whom a participation in the pastoral care of a parish is to be entrusted in accord with canon 517, §2.

The following procedures are intended to provide a foundation upon which dioceses may develop their own policies with

---

Catholic Social Teaching and the American Economy," *Origins* 16 (November 27, 1986) 409–455.

3. Ibid., 446, n. 347.

4. National Association of Church Personnel Administrators, *Just Treatment for Those Who Work for the Church* (Cincinnati: NACPA, 1986) ix.

5. Ibid., 7–10.

regard to the appointment, evaluation, and retention of parish directors. The establishment of procedures on a diocesan level serves to minimize tensions and disputes and forestalls perceptions of arbitrariness in decision-making in individual cases.[6]

Surfacing and Interviewing Candidates

After having established the position description and required qualifications for a parish director, a process by which qualified individuals will be considered for appointment needs to be developed. The diocese could either proceed to a recruitment, interview, and appointment process each time a parish director position arises at a parish or the diocese could establish a pool of candidates from which appointments to this office can be made as the need arises. There are advantages and disadvantages to each system.

In the former system, the general position description could be tailored with specific details based upon the individual parish and its needs. Any special qualifications in candidates, such as facility in a given language, could be taken into account when the opening of the position is announced. In this system candidates would only come forward when there is a specific need for a parish director in a given situation.

The second system also has its own advantages. By allowing a prior screening process, the diocese can begin establishing a larger pool of candidates from which future appointments will be made. These persons would already have been judged as meeting the minimal standards and criteria for appointment, such as background, formation, and pastoral experience. They would not relinquish current employment merely by joining the ranks of those determined to be qualified for appointment; diocesan policy should make clear that individuals do not jeopardize current

6. Robert T. Kennedy, "Commentary," in *Protection of Rights of Persons in the Church: Revised Report of the Canon Law Society of America on the Subject of Due Process* (Washington: Canon Law Society of America, 1991) 50.

positions by making application for future consideration as parish directors. This latter system is more closely parallel to present practice in most dioceses with regard to assignment of ordained ministers to pastoral positions.

Application Process

Upon determination by the diocesan bishop that a need currently exists or will exist in the foreseeable future for appointment of parish directors in the diocese, the position description for that office should be prepared and approved. The qualifications required in a parish director should be ascertained based upon that description.

Decisions will need to be made by the bishop and his personnel advisors regarding the scope of the search process for the person(s) who will be considered for the role of parish director. Based upon that decision, resources for ministry listings on the local, regional, and national level should be utilized. Such listing should clearly specify whether the application process is being undertaken for consideration of appointment to a specific position or for inclusion in a pool of candidates from which future appointments will be made.

The diocesan bishop may find it helpful to establish a special committee to whom he will commit the responsibility for screening and interviewing prospective candidates for the office of parish director. Such a committee may be composed of the following:

a. a representative from the diocesan office for human resources or personnel office;

b. a representative from the priests personnel board or the diocesan office for clergy;

c. a representative from among existing lay pastoral ministers or parish directors;

d. a representative from among priest supervisors or sacramental ministers currently working with parish directors;

e. other membership or resource personnel as determined by the diocesan bishop.

The membership of this committee could determine who among themselves or among available support personnel will receive candidates' applications and track completion of the application process.

Prospective candidates should be referred to the appropriate office or agency, e.g., the diocesan office for human resources, a personnel board, or a parish director screening committee, for further information and application requirements. (See Appendix A for sample application and list of requirements in the application process.)

Screening Applicants

As prospective candidates complete the application process, appropriate documentation should be made available to the screening committee. It is the responsibility of the screening committee to determine which applicants warrant further consideration. Those who are deemed ineligible for consideration should be notified promptly by the designated representative of the screening committee. In most cases, it would seem appropriate to indicate in which areas the applicant's resume or qualifications were insufficient for further consideration.

Interview

Those applicants who are judged eligible for further consideration as candidates for the position of parish director should be notified and arrangements made for an interview with the screening and interview committee. The coordination of the interview process could be assumed by the same person designated above to direct the application stage.

The interview process should be directed toward narrowing the field of candidates either to the general pool of parish directors or to the one or two most qualified for the specific position to be filled. The interview should be directed in such a way that the candidate's gifts and skills can best be matched to the general or specific needs of the position. Interview questions and style of interviewing should be determined in advance by the screening and interview committee.

Selection of Nominees

If a diocese has chosen to select a general pool of candidates from which specific parish director appointments will be made, then as positions are established or become vacant, nominees from among the members of the pool will need to be surfaced. Once there is identification of the specific parish(es), the selection and interview process can become more focussed.

Parish Assessment

Each parish as a specific community of the Christian faithful (c. 515, §1) has its own unique characteristics, pastoral programs, and leadership needs. These identifying elements should be taken into consideration in the process of appointment of pastoral leadership, both clerical and lay. As part of the determination of whether a pastor or parish director shall be appointed to a specific parish, a parish assessment should be undertaken.

The parish assessment process should include the following:

a. interviews with present pastoral staff;
b. on-site visitation;
c. consultation with parish pastoral council;
d. open parish meeting.

The purpose of the assessment process is not to move toward a "congregational" model of ministry assignments whereby parish leadership positions are determined and filled by the local community; rather, the process involves the parish community in refining and describing its own identity. The parish's self-expression in word, worship, service, and administration will help determine the qualities and skills needed in the individual who will assume a position of pastoral leadership within the community.

The assessment process can be conducted by a member of the priests personnel board as part of its usual responsibilities. In those instances in which a parish director rather than a pastor will be appointed for the first time at a given parish, issues related to this decision should be handled with the parish by a diocesan representative prior to the appointment process. It should not be among the responsibilities of a parish director to facilitate the remote preparation of a community for this change in leadership.

Open Listing Among Approved Candidates

If the diocese has a pool of candidates already screened and judged qualified for the position of parish director, information about a parish which has a vacancy could be distributed among those candidates. Most dioceses already have mechanisms in place by which they publicize or "open list" parishes for clergy assignments. Consideration should be given to establishing a parallel system when the appointment of a parish director is warranted.

Interviewing Applicants

The screening and interview committee (see above I, A) reviews the credentials and experiences of the candidates who have come forward for consideration for the specific appointment, attempting to match the candidates to the needs of the parish. Based on these considerations, the committee would contact those candidates who are being considered for appointment and arrange for interviews. The interview would focus on the ability of the candidate to respond to the assessed needs of the parish. Since this interview concerns an already specified parish, its content can be tailored to the concerns of the committee and the candidate with regard to the designated parish.

Decision-Making Process and Presentation for Appointment

The role of the interview and selection committee would need to be determined by the diocesan bishop. He could use their services in a manner similar to that of many priests personnel boards. As a result of their consideration of the gifts and skills of the candidates in light of the needs of the parish, their deliberations would result in the placing of candidates' names before the bishop for his final approval and appointment. It may serve the bishop well to have this committee present candidates in a priority order, ranking them according to suitability for the appointment to be made. Supportive documentation and/or summaries of the committee's recommendations regarding individuals would be appropriate especially in those cases in which the bishop does not know the candidates personally. Depending upon local circumstances, input from parish representation could be included in the documentation as could the recommendation of the priest supervisor if he is already identified.

Appointment to Office

The position of parish director fulfills the criteria set forth in canon 145, §1 for an ecclesiastical office. Those lay persons to whom a participation in the pastoral care of a parish is to be entrusted in accord with canon 517, §2 become ecclesiastical office holders by reason of their appointment. The general provisions of the 1983 code on ecclesiastical office (cc. 145–156) are applicable to the office of parish director. The details of what constitutes this particular office do not appear in the universal legislation, however. It would be incumbent upon the diocesan bishop to constitute the specifics of such an office by means of particular legislation or by means of an administrative decree. Such designation regarding the office should include:

a. position description which defines the office;
b. required qualifications in the office holder;
c. process for selection and appointment;
d. rights and obligations attached to the office;
e. term of office;
f. cause for and means of termination from office.[7]

With regard to the general canonical provisions pertaining to ecclesiastical office, several would bear examination in relation to this current study.

Authority to Appoint

Among the means by which provision of an ecclesiastical office may occur, the one applicable for a parish director appears to be free conferral (cc. 147; 157). It is the diocesan bishop who has the authority to make such an appointment. This exercise of his pastoral office is consistent with his authority to appoint pastors (c. 523). It is the bishop who makes the initial determination that a participation in the pastoral care of a parish is to be entrusted to someone other than a pastor and it is the diocesan bishop who appoints the priest supervisor in such a situation (c. 517, §2). Obviously the bishop has the discretionary authority to consult with those whom he feels can best advise him about such an appointment. Such advisors might include the priests personnel board, the vicar forane (dean) of the vacant parish, and a selection and interview committee as noted above.

Letter of Appointment

Following the general norm that the provision of office is to be made in writing (c. 156), the diocesan bishop should communicate his assignment of a parish director in a letter of appointment. This letter of appointment should specify not only the parish to

---

7. For a similar analysis with regard to establishment of offices by particular law, see James F. Parizek, "Ecclesiastical Office," in *Clergy Procedural Handbook,* ed. R. Calvo and N. Klinger (Washington: CLSA, 1992) 111.

which the appointment is made but also the term of office, the effective date for assuming the office, and any specific mandates or expectations with regard to the fulfillment of the office. Because of the close working relationship that will need to be established and maintained between the parish director and the priest supervisor, the name of the individual assigned to fulfill the latter position should also be indicated in the letter of appointment. Reference should be made to the fulfillment of their respective position descriptions in each of their letters of appointment.

The letter of appointment should also include the designation of any special authorizations being granted to the parish director. (See appropriate section of this present manual.) Indication of the lines of authority and accountability should also be mentioned as well as reference to the system of evaluation. (See Appendix B for sample of appointment letter.)

Announcement of Appointment

Because of the significance of the appointment of a parish director both for the life of the parish and of the diocese, consideration should be given to the means by which the appointment is announced publicly. If there is a system in place for the announcement of appointments of pastors, the same system should be utilized for the announcement of a parish director. If parishes whose pastoral care is entrusted to a parish director are not to have the impression that they are somehow "second class" parishes, as many processes as possible which are parallel to the appointment of a pastor should be used. In dioceses which have a diocesan newspaper or other official means of communication, appointments of pastors are often announced publicly through that medium; the same vehicle could be used for the public announcement of the appointment of a parish director. A formal announcement should also be conveyed from the bishop to the concerned parish.

Installation in Office

When a pastor is appointed to a parish, following the method established by particular law or legitimate custom, the local ordinary or his delegate is ordinarily to install that person in office (c. 527, §2) There is nothing in the law which would require that a parish director be installed in the office to which he or she has been appointed. However, there is also nothing in the law that would preclude the development and use of an installation ceremony. It would seem appropriate that the local ordinary or the person usually delegated by him for the installation of pastors be designated for the installation of parish directors as well. If a regional episcopal vicar or vicar forane is in place it might be appropriate for him to conduct the installation. (See Appendix C for sample ceremony.)

Evaluation Process

Once the parish director is appointed, a means of performance evaluation should be undertaken at regular intervals. This performance evaluation should directly correlate to the position description. Various instruments for this process of evaluation are available and in use by dioceses.[8] Whatever system of evaluation is chosen, based on local need and practice, the following elements should be taken into consideration:

a. relationship between position description and evaluation;

b. person(s) authorized for or involved in the evaluation process;

c. correlation between evaluation and renewal/termination of contract, renewal of term or termination from office;

d. effect of evaluation on salary;

e. establishment of evaluation schedule;

f. access to evaluation results;

g. right to and process of recourse against evaluation results.

8. The National Association for Church Personnel Administrators is an excellent source for assistance in the development or review of evaluation instruments.

Loss of Office/Renewal in Office

Stability is one of the attributes of an ecclesiastical office. Therefore, canonical provisions exist to help ensure that individuals holding office are not summarily removed from office or their positions terminated without process. At the same time, since the good of the community demands quality pastoral leadership, those who have the responsibility to oversee the pastoral mission of the diocese need provisions which allow for removal from office of those who are not contributing to the good of the community. On the other hand, if the needed pastoral leadership is being provided and conditions have not significantly altered, there needs to be a system by which the office holder's term can be renewed. As pastoral conditions within a diocese change, there may be a need to transfer pastoral leaders from one setting to another; a defined process for such transfer should exist within the diocese in order to guarantee that both individual rights and the common good are protected.

Loss of Office in General

Loss of ecclesiastical office is treated in canons 184–196. Loss of office occurs through:

a. expiration of the term for which one was appointed;
b. reaching of retirement age;
c. resignation from office;
d. transfer to another office;
e. removal from office;
f. penal privation of office.

The practical application of the general canonical norms on loss of office to the position of the parish director warrants examination.

Expiration of Term/Retirement

If a parish director is appointed with a specified term of office, then upon completion of that predetermined time period the office is lost (c. 184). This loss of office only takes effect, however, upon written notification of the expiration of the term (c. 186). Therefore, at the diocesan level appropriate record keeping should track the terms of office of parish directors in order to ensure that sufficient time is allowed to evaluate the parish situation upon expiration of the term.

When the term of office of a parish director is ready to expire, it would be beneficial to provide a process by which decisions can be made about the future pastoral leadership in the parish. Since the appointment of parish directors occurs only when there are insufficient numbers of priests to fulfill the office of pastor, the assessment of the status of the diocese in terms of available priests could be reviewed at the time a parish director's term expires. Conditions which led to the choice of a particular parish for assignment of a parish director may have altered during the time period in which the parish director functioned. Therefore, this may also be an appropriate time to assess the current needs of the parish.

Upon completion of the local and diocesan assessment, decisions about future staffing of the parish can be made. Options include continuation of the position of parish director at the parish or the assignment of a priest as pastor. In the former case, the incumbent parish director may be considered for a renewal of the term of office after appropriate evaluation of the fulfillment of the position description. Alternately, there may be the appointment of the parish director to another parish needing such leadership and the assignment of a new parish director to the present parish. As dioceses increase the number of experienced parish directors, their movement from one parish to another may decrease the need for recruitment and screening of qualified candidates.

There is no universal law establishing a mandatory retirement age for a parish director. Diocesan guidelines or particular law could establish such a directive. It may be appropriate to establish a norm parallel to that which governs the mandatory retirement of pastors at age 75 (c. 538, §3). Upon reaching an established age for retirement the parish director would submit a letter of resignation to the diocesan bishop. With the acceptance of the resignation, the retirement of the parish director becomes effective on the date stated in the letter of acceptance. Provisions to fulfill the individual's canonical right to an adequate pension, social security, and health benefits need to be kept in mind at the time of retirement (canon 231, §2).

Resignation from Office

In addition to a resignation submitted at the time of retirement, a parish director may resign for other reasons. The office is lost by means of such a resignation. Such a resignation must be free, cannot be unjustly coerced, and must be based on a just cause (c. 188). Resignation from the office of parish director takes place by means of written or oral communication of that fact to the diocesan bishop (c. 189).

Examples of just cause for such a resignation would include ill health, required relocation, family commitments, inability to fulfill the position requirements. Because of the newness of the position of parish director and the need for dioceses to grow in their lived experience of dealing with the issues related to this position, it would be advisable for an "exit interview" to take place at the time of a resignation. This interview would include an assessment by the resigning parish director of the adequacy of support systems for the fulfillment of the office, an evaluation of the current parish needs, an analysis of the successes and failures in the working relationship between the parish director and the priest supervisor with due regard for the sacramental priest who may also serve in the parish. An exit interview could also be used to evaluate the role of the diocese in relation to these newly emerging pastoral ministers. The exit interview need not be conducted by the diocesan bishop himself but the results should be communicated to him and to others who assist him in overseeing the pastoral care of the diocese.

Process of Transfer

As the conditions within a diocese alter and pastoral needs shift, there may be situations in which a diocesan bishop would choose to transfer a parish director from one parish to another or from the office of parish director to another office over which he has authority (c. 190, §1). If there are sufficient numbers of qualified parish directors present within a diocese, a system may be established whereby the individuals make known to the bishop their willingness to be transferred from a current position to a newly opened parish directorship.

Should grave cause such as pastoral necessity dictate, the diocesan bishop may need to transfer a parish director to another parish or to another office even if the individual is unwilling. Canon 190, §2 requires that the unwilling transfer of an office holder be enacted according to legal process. There are no procedures for transfers of parish directors established in the universal law. In order to protect individual rights and assure the common good, it would be appropriate to establish a process for such transfer on a diocesan basis. The norms for transfer of pastors (cc. 1748–1752) could serve well as guides for the development of such a process. The key elements to be considered in the establishment of such a process would include:

a. Assessment of needs—it is the responsibility of the diocesan bishop to determine that there is sufficient pastoral need to warrant a transfer. Appropriate avenues for consultation on the parish, regional, and diocesan level should be established as part of the assessment process (cf. c. 1748);

b. Communication with parish director—the diocesan bishop presents the proposed transfer in writing to the parish director indicating the persuasive reasons for such a consideration (cf. c. 1748);

c. Opportunity for response—the parish director should be free to present opposing reasons which would argue against consideration of such a transfer; such a response should be communicated in writing (cf. c. 1749);

d. Consultation—if the transfer is not readily accepted, the diocesan bishop should consult with his advisors (e.g., designated representative from the parish director screening and interview committee), weighing the pro's and con's of the transfer (cf. c. 1750);

e. Communication of final decision—upon completion of the assessment and consultation process the diocesan bishop should communicate the decision to the parish director in writing for the validity of that decision (cf. cc. 190, §3; 1751).

The establishment of a well defined procedure for transfer would go far to ensure that the "good of souls" remains the primary consideration (c. 1752) and that the right of the individual to just treatment is protected.

Process of Removal/Privation

Despite every effort to surface appropriate candidates, to appoint qualified individuals, to provide necessary support systems in ministry, and to undertake sufficient evaluation procedures, situations may arise which necessitate the removal of a parish director from office. Removal from this office takes place either by decree of the diocesan bishop or by the law itself (c. 192).

When there has been an undefined term or prior to the expiration of a designated term, the diocesan bishop can remove a parish director from office only for grave reasons (c. 193, §§1 & 2). The law also guarantees the parish director the right to due process in the removal (c. 193, §§1 & 2). The universal law does not designate sufficient cause for removal or establish a process for removal from the office of parish director. Therefore, it is incumbent upon the diocesan bishop to designate causes and establish such a process locally.

The parish director is appointed to provide, as much as is canonically possible, for the pastoral care of the parish. Given the fact that the "good of souls is the supreme law of the Church" (c. 1752), the gravity of reasons for removal of the parish director should be commensurate with the impact on the community and the individual that such a removal effects. In delineating reasons which could lead to removal from the office of parish director, the diocesan bishop could refer to the reasons which are considered appropriate for the removal of a pastor from office. A sample list of such reasons is found in canon 1741:

a. a manner of acting which is judged to be seriously detrimental or disturbing to ecclesiastical communion;

b. an incapacitating physical or mental condition precluding appropriate fulfillment of pastoral responsibilities;

c. loss of reputation within the parish community or enduring aversion by parishioners;

d. serious neglect or violation of responsibilities related to one's office, which persist even after a warning;

e. poor fiscal management resulting in damage to the Church which cannot be remedied in any other way.

When there is evidence that reasons which would lead to removal exist, the parish director should first be notified of the problems and be given the opportunity to effect the necessary changes. If there are no signs of improvement, the good of the community may require that the bishop initiate a process of removal.

The process as established by the diocesan bishop should be followed carefully. Using the canonical process for the removal of a pastor (cc. 1742 ff.) as a guide, the process instituted by the diocesan bishop should include the following elements:

a. Investigation of problems—as soon as serious deficiencies in the life or ministry of the parish director are brought to the attention of the bishop or his delegate for such matters, efforts should be made to determine the reliability of the reports and the accuracy of their content;

b. Communication of deficiencies—when it is determined that there is substance to the reports, the bishop or his delegate should communicate with the parish director regarding the serious problems and outline remedial actions which are to be taken;

c. Right of defense—the parish director should be given the opportunity to present a defense against the reported deficiencies;

d. Decree of removal—if the diocesan bishop, after appropriate consultation, determines that inadequate remediation has occurred or that the deficiency is so serious that immediate action is warranted, a written communication of removal is to be sent to the parish director for the validity of the decision.

In addition to the removal from office by decree, a parish director could lose office by the law itself. Given the focus of our attention in this present study, that is, the parish director who is canonically a lay person, only one *ipso iure* removal is applicable. Canon 194, §1, 2° states that a person who has publicly defected from the Church or from the communion of the Church is removed from ecclesiastical office by the law itself. However, the provisions of the second paragraph of the same canon would require that the facts of the case be established by the diocesan bishop and that he declare the *ipso iure* removal by decree.

Privation of office is a type of removal that occurs as a penalty for an offense (c. 196). The norms on the penal process (cc. 1341–1353; 1717–1731) are to be followed in such a case. Furthermore, since privation of office is a perpetual expiatory penalty, a judicial penal process is warranted (c. 1242, §2).[9] The adherence to these norms supports the right of the parish director not to have canonical penalties imposed without due process (c. 221, §3).

Removal from office does not terminate all of the rights of the parish director in relation to the office from which he or she was terminated. Rights arising from an employment contract would remain intact for the duration of the contract (c. 192). Such rights may include salary and/or benefits according to the provisions of the contract. Furthermore, removal of the parish director by decree does not absolve the diocesan bishop from financial oblig-

9. For a succinct and thorough exposition on the penal process, see Gregory Ingels, "Processes Which Govern the Application of Penalties," in *Clergy Procedural Handbook,* 206–237.

ations if that office was the source of the individual's financial support (c. 195). The bishop must see that support is provided to the individual for a suitable period of time unless other provisions are made. Such provisions should be clearly stated in the employment contract, the position description, or diocesan policy.

Appendix A

Sample Application Form for Position of Parish Director

Arch/diocese of _____

Name _____

Address _____

_____

Telephone _____

Religious Community (if applicable) _____

Education

Degree	*Year*	*Educational Institutions*	*Major Field*

Work Experience

Dates	*Position*	*Place*	*Contact Person*

Professional Involvement/Continuing Education

Date	*Place*	*Description*

Please include with this application the following documentation:

1. Sacramental records
2. Letter of recommendation from Pastor
3. Statement of interest in and understanding of the position of Parish Director
4. Statement of support from spouse/religious superior (as applicable)
5. List of references

Appendix B

Sample Appointment Letter

Office of the Bishop of _____

Dear (*Parish Director*),

By means of this letter I appoint you to the office of Parish Director of (*Parish*). Your roles and responsibilities are described in the attached position description. I also extend to you the authorizations which are listed in the enclosed document.

This appointment is effective (*Date*) and is for a term of (*Number*) years. In fulfilling your role as Parish Director you will work with Father (*Name*) as priest supervisor. (If applicable: Father (*Name*) will provide sacramental ministry to the parish.)

Please contact my office to arrange an appropriate date for your installation ceremony in the parish. This appointment will be announced publicly in the parish on (*Date*).

(Appropriate personal and concluding remarks)

_____   _____
Bishop   Notary

(Seal)

Appendix C

Sample Installation Ceremony for Parish Director

Ideally the diocesan bishop or his delegate should be present and preside over the installation ceremony. Other participants in the liturgical action could include the parish council chairperson, the priest supervisor, the sacramental minister if appropriate, a representative from the religious community if the parish director is a religious, and the parish director's spouse if the person is married.

Installation:

The bishop (or delegate) greets the community and offers some brief remarks on the significance of the installation ceremony. He then addresses the new Parish Director.

BISHOP: (*Name of Parish Director*), will you serve the people of (*Parish*) by living to the best of your ability the life of faith demanded by the Gospel and by fulfilling your role as Parish Director?

PARISH DIRECTOR: I will.

BISHOP: Will you serve the needs of this community through the ministries of Word, Worship, Service, and Administration in accord with your responsibilities as Parish Director?

PARISH DIRECTOR: I will.

BISHOP: Will you work with the members of this community, the priest(s) who will assist with their pastoral care, your priest supervisor, and me/your bishop, to promote a spirit of shared responsibility and respect for one another?

PARISH DIRECTOR: I will.

The bishop (or delegate) addresses the congregation:

BISHOP: Members of (*Parish*), will you receive (*Parish Director*) as your Parish Director and give him/her the support of your prayers and your cooperation?

PEOPLE: We will.

BISHOP: (*Parish Director*), you have expressed your willingness to serve as Parish Director of (*Parish*).

I invite you now to receive these symbols of your ministry.

(Representatives from the community come forward with a Bible, bowl of water, parish mission statement, financial records. As each gift is presented, the Parish Director receives it and responds to the bishop as follows:)

Scripture:

BISHOP: Receive this copy of the Sacred Scriptures, the story of our salvation.

PARISH DIRECTOR: In a spirit of humility, I receive this Book of Scriptures. May I proclaim and live its message in this community so that our lives will be governed by God's holy word.

Bowl of Water:

BISHOP: Receive this sign of our common baptism in the Lord.

PARISH DIRECTOR: I joyfully receive this symbol of baptism. May I continually call forth the gifts of this baptized community in service to one another.

Parish Mission Statement:

BISHOP: Accept the mission statement of this parish community which describes their calling as followers of Christ.

PARISH DIRECTOR: I welcome this mission statement as an expression of the vision of this community and their desire to be united in heart and purpose.

Financial Records:

BISHOP: Receive the financial records of this parish in which the gifts of this community are counted and recorded.

PARISH DIRECTOR: In a spirit of stewardship I accept these records as a sign of the generosity of God's people and of my service of administration within this community.

(The Parish Director kneels before the bishop who, with his hands extended and inviting all present to do the same, imparts his blessing.)

BISHOP: My brothers and sisters, pray with me that God will give his blessings to (*Parish Director*) who has been chosen for ministry within this community.

Loving God, Source of all we have and are, we praise you.

Give your blessing to (*Parish Director*) that he/she may be an instrument of your care for the people of this parish.

By his/her life and faith may he/she show forth your Word of Truth and celebrate your presence in love and joy.

Through prayer and good works may he/she grow in knowledge of you.

May he/she call forth the gifts of this community, allowing others to offer their services and to minister as they have been called to do.

We make our prayer through Jesus Christ your Son, our Lord, who lives and reigns with you and the Holy Spirit, one God, forever and ever.

ALL: Amen.

Appendix D

Sample Contract I: Parish Lay Employment Agreement

In this sample contract, the parish is identified as the employer of the parish director. It is a standard parish employee contract and exemplifies "at will" employment agreements. Civil counsel should be consulted for applicable civil norms and advice before a diocese determines the form of contract to be utilized with a parish director.

Arch/Diocese of _____

Parish Lay Employment Agreement

This agreement is made and entered into in the State of _____, County of _____, this _____ day of _____, 19____ between the parish of _____, hereafter referred to as "employer" and (*parish director*), hereafter referred to as "employee."

1. Nature of Agreement

The employer hereby employs the employee as parish director for the parish of _____. Employee agrees to perform faithfully, industriously and ethically to the best of the employee's ability, experience, Catholic religious training and talents those duties set forth in the job description attached as "Exhibit A" hereto and initialed by the parties and made part of this agreement. Employee agrees to perform those duties at the times and places specified by the employer.

2. Duration

Unless sooner terminated in accordance with the provision of paragraph 5 below, this agreement and the employee's rights, duties and responsibilities shall commence as of the _____ day of _____, 19____ and shall terminate on the _____ day of _____, 19____.

3. *Compensation and Benefits*

a) Employee shall receive full payment of all services to be performed under this contract a mutually agreed sum of _____ per _____ which shall be paid to employee in equal biweekly installments subject to all legal and contractual deductions including those for and by federal and state laws and regulations.

b) Employee shall also receive, during the term of this agreement, all other benefits including medical and hospitalization insurance coverage as provided for lay employees of the Arch/diocese of _____ Employee Handbook and which said benefits are subject to change, modification or reduction from time to time within the discretion of the Arch/diocese of _____.

4. *Automobile Expenses and Insurance*

a) If the employee is to use his or her automobile in the course of the employee's work, the employer shall reimburse employee for the use of his or her private automobile at the rate which from time to time is currently being reimbursed to employees and clergy of the Arch/diocese of _____ for travel associated with employee's work excluding regular travel to and from work.

b) Employee shall obtain and maintain during the existence of this agreement, liability insurance on the automobile he or she uses to perform the duties set forth in the job description annexed hereto. That insurance shall contain such minimal limits of liability as are required by the Arch/diocese of _____ from time to time and verification thereof shall be given to the employer in writing.

c) Employer shall reimburse employee for travel expenses, including meals and lodging away from residence, provided such expenses are associated with his or her work, are approved by the employer in advance of the expenditures and appropriate receipts of expenditures are submitted to employer.

5. *Termination*

a) This agreement shall be terminated by either employer or employee without cause and for any reason upon thirty days advance written notice to the employee. Upon termination all terms and conditions of this agreement for cause shall include but not be limited to the following:

1) failure to comply with the terms of this agreement or the policies and procedures of the employer;

2) incompetence, neglect of duty, immorality, default of character, public scandal or other circumstances that would render employee unsuitable for continued employment;

3) inability of the employee, for whatever reason, to perform the essential functions of his or her assigned duties at the times and places specified by the employer for a period of at least forty-five (45) consecutive days or more than sixty (60) days in the aggregate in any twelve (12) months period from the date of this agreement.

6. *Renewal*

This agreement shall be automatically renewed for an additional period of one (1) year, commencing on the day following the completion of the term of this agreement as set forth in paragraph 2 except and unless on or before the first day of April of each year either party hereto shall notify the other party hereto of his or her intention not to renew the agreement for the ensuing term. If the agreement is not signed by April 15, it is understood that the employee does not choose to continue this agreement and said agreement shall terminate in all respects.

7. *Renegotiation*

This agreement and the attached job description may be renegotiated each year on or before the first day of April.

8. *Contractural Disputes*

This agreement shall be construed in accordance with the laws of the State of _____. If any disputes arise between the two parties to this agreement which cannot be amicably resolved between them, then any and all such disputes whether arising out of this agreement or out of the employment relationship created hereby shall be determined solely and exclusively through arbitration proceedings to be conducted pursuant to the rules of the American Arbitration Association.

The terms of this agreement are hereby accepted and executed by the undersigned on the date set forth below.

_____   _____

Employer   Date

_____   _____

Employee   Date

Sample Contract II: Parish Director Contract

In this sample contract, the arch/diocese is identified as the employer of the parish director with the parish as the paying agent. This contract includes a "for cause" provision for termination. Civil counsel should be consulted for applicable civil norms and advice before a diocese determines the form of contract to be utilized with a parish director.

Contract for Parish Director

Arch/Diocese of _____

This contract is made this _____ day of _____, 19____, by and between the Arch/diocese of _____ (hereafter referred to as Employer) and _____ (hereafter referred to as Employee).

1. The Employer agrees to hire the above-named person as parish director of _____ Parish, in (*city/town*), for the period beginning (*date*) and ending (*date*).

The Employer further agrees to provide a salary of $_____, payable by the assigned Parish, in equal installments, on the _____ day(s) of each and every month, for the term of this contract (subject to the termination provisions set forth below), and subject to payroll deductions required by law and other authorized deductions. Notwithstanding that the assigned Parish will pay the salary to the Employee, it is agreed that such payments are at all times on behalf of the Arch/diocese as the sole employer, and at no time shall Employee be considered to be an employee of the assigned parish.

2. In addition to the annual salary, the Employee shall be entitled to the benefits as provided for in the attached benefit supplement of this contract, which is incorporated herein by reference and made a part hereof. The Employee hereby accepts the

terms of this contract and agrees to diligently perform the services described in the position description supplement of this contract, which is incorporated herein and made a part hereof, and to devote his or her full time and attention to the performance of his or her duties hereunder. The Employee, in the performance of the services agreed to in this contract will be accountable to the Arch/bishop of the Arch/diocese of _____ or his designee.

3. This contract is made for a three year period. If either party does not wish to renew the contract, notice in writing shall be given to the other party at least thirty (30) days before the expiration of this contract. If notice of non-renewal is not given, the contract shall automatically renew for a period of one year on the same terms and conditions existing herein, and shall be renewed for additional one year periods if notice not to renew is not given thirty (30) days prior to expiration of any renewed contract. The Employer agrees that the Employee shall not be discharged during the term of this contract without good and sufficient cause, which shall be determined solely by the Arch/bishop of _____. In the case of such discharge, the Employer's obligations hereunder shall cease as of the date of such discharge. This contract can be terminated by the mutual agreement of both parties, in which case the responsibilities of each party shall cease. This agreement shall also be terminated by the death, or total disability, of Employee.

4. It is agreed that, solely at the option of the Arch/diocese of _____, the Employee may be reassigned to a different Parish during the term of this agreement to perform the duties of Parish Director in accordance with the attached position description. It is also agreed that the Employee may be assigned additional duties or duties different from those contained in the attached position description, so long as they are substantially related to the duties contained in the attached position description.

5. This contract is made solely between the two undersigned parties and constitutes the entire understanding with respect to the subject matter herein. There are no restrictions, promises, covenants, or undertakings other than those expressly set forth or incorporated by reference herein. This contract supersedes all prior negotiations, agreements, and undertakings between the parties with respect to such subject matter. This agreement may only be modified in writing signed by the parties and may not be modified orally.

_____

Parish Director (Employee)

_____

Arch/bishop of _____ (Employer)

Date: _____

Select Annotated Bibliography

Beeman, Dennis, et. al. *Pastoral Coordinators: Parish Leadership without a Resident Pastor.* New York: National Pastoral Life Center, 1995. This 16 page document is part of a series of "Center Papers" addressing various contemporary issues affecting pastoral life. The paper summarizes findings from a 1993 conference convened to address practical situations affecting parish life when there is no (resident) pastor. Background, qualifications, selection process, and ministry components considered by different dioceses in the appointment of personnel under the provision of c. 517, §2 are presented, frequently in the form of charts.

Burkart, Gary. *The Parish Life Coordinator.* Kansas City, MO: Sheed and Ward, 1992. This book is based on the lived experiences of pastoral personnel and parishioners where c. 517, §2 has been implemented. The author brings his expertise in the field of social science to bear on the data and draws conclusions regarding the successes and shortcomings of the various projects. For those seeking to design policies and procedures around c. 517, §2 there will be less interest in the charts and figures on data and more interest in some of the conclusions drawn from that empirical information.

Chandler, Mary Moisson. *The Pastoral Associate and the Lay Pastor.* Collegeville, MN: The Liturgical Press, 1986. This brief (83 page) booklet is based primarily on the experience and policies of the Archdiocese of Portland. While canonists may not find the oversimplification of complex canonical issues helpful (including some terminology and conclusions), the summaries of parochial, ministerial needs may assist in defining areas for pastoral care.

Euart, Sharon, R.S.M. *Pastoral Coordinators and Canon Law.* New York: National Pastoral Life Center, 1995. Another in the "Center Papers" series, this 10 page document (also published as an article in *The Jurist* 54 (1994) 369–386) addresses specific canonical concerns related to c. 517, §2 within the larger context of Vatican II and the canonical understanding of parish. The implications for diocesan and parish leadership in implementing this canonical provision are also addressed.

Klister, Roy. *Non-Presbyteral Pastoral Care in Parish Liturgical Life.* Wrightstown, WI: R.M. Klister, 1991. As an expanded and reworked dissertation presented to the Liturgical Institute of San Anselmo, the content of this work is more clearly focused on liturgical issues of c. 517, §2. Canonical issues are raised and addressed as well.

Monette, Maurice, O.M.I. *Partners in Ministry: Priests in Collaboration with Parish Life Coordinators.* Kansas City, MO: Sheed and Ward, 1988. This small booklet (62 pages) was published as a follow up to a 1988 symposium sponsored by the Institute for Pastoral Life. Rather than address theoretical issues, the booklet focuses on the attitudinal adjustments needed by priests who will function under the provisions of c. 517, §2. The text includes accounts from the personal experiences of priests who have assumed the role of "priest supervisor" and suggestions for future application flow from these experiences. Reflection questions on various topics make this a practical tool for those preparing for or involved in implementation of c. 517, §2.

Murnion, Philip, et. al. *New Parish Ministers.* New York: National Pastoral Life Center, 1992. This book is the published study commissioned by the NCCB for the purpose of examining the situation of lay persons in parish ministry positions. Only passing reference is made to the application of c. 517, §2. The findings, however, drawn from both quantitative and qualitative research, may be of assistance to those who are considering the impact of parish directors within the general context of lay ministry in the Church in the U.S.

Vadakumthala, Alexander. *Lay Person as Caretaker of a Parish.* Rome: Pontifical Urban University, 1992. This sizable doctoral dissertation approaches the application of c. 517, §2 from both a theoretical and practical perspective. Of particular interest will be the research into the lived experience of particular churches on four continents.

Contributors

Barbara Anne Cusack, J.C.D., is chancellor of the Archdiocese of Milwaukee, Wisconsin.

Therese Guerin Sullivan, S.P., D.Min., J.C.L., is a judge of the marriage tribunal and liaison to women and men religious of the Diocese of Gary, Indiana.